Players

Players

Poems by Michael D. Riley

Turning Point

Published by Turning Point
P.O. Box 541106
Cincinnati, OH 45254-1106

ISBN: 9781934999356
LCCN: 2008909683

Poetry Editor: Kevin Walzer
Business Editor: Lori Jareo

Visit us on the web at www.turningpointbooks.com

"Behold, I have played the fool, and erred exceedingly."
—Samuel 26: 22

"Fate wrote her [Princess Caroline] a most tremendous tragedy, and she played it in tights."
—Max Beerbohm

"Then I thought of the tribe whose dances never fail
   For they keep dancing till they sight the deer."
—Seamus Heaney,
"Station Island IX"
Station Island

Acknowledgments

A number of the poems in this collection had the good fortune to find prior publication. Those initial appearances: "Macrame," *The Arizona Quarterly* [reprinted in *Anthology of Magazine Verse and Yearbook of American Poetry*]; "Gymnast," *The Atlanta Review*; "Grandma On Wash Day," *Beyond Doggerel*; "In the Old Way," *Birmingham Poetry Review;* "Epitaph," *California Quarterly*; "Apologia: Uncle Fitz," *Creeping Bent*; "Ballet Lesson," "Groundhog," "In the Garden," "The Reader," "The Visit," *Cumberland Poetry Review*; "Conditional," *Earth's Daughters*; "Old Airman," *Edge City Review*; "Why There Are So Many Murders at the Post Office," *EDGZ*; "St. Francis by the Lower Lavatory: St. Joseph-in-the-Hills Retreat House," *Ekphrasis*; "Those Who Go Gently," *Farmer's Market;* "Bear," *Flyway* [formerly *Poet and Critic*]; "Adam's Death," *Great River Review*; "Seven-Eleven," *Home Planet News*; "Shell Game," "One Body," *Iron Horse Literary Review*; "Photograph of Bergen-Belsen, 1945," *Karamu* [reprinted in *Blood to Remember: American Poets on the Holocaust*, 2nd Edition]; "Drum," *Midland Review*; "Amish Farmer," *New Rag Rising*; "Kumbh Mela," *New Virginia Review*; "An Absence of Whales," *No Exit*; "Chinese Lanterns," *Parting Gifts*; "Late Afternoon," *Pemmican*; "My Mother and John Keats," *Plains Poetry Journal*; "Betsy Fishman," *Poetpourri*; "Regret," "Snow Man," *Poetry*; "Lucy," "House Sparrows in October," *Poetry Ireland Review*; "Operation," *Poets On: Healing*; "DMW-HLW," *Portland Review*; "Whale Rood," *Riversedge*; "Lift," *Runes*; "Old Wood," *Separate Doors*; "The Winners," *Slant*; "Three Emigrations," *The Small Pond Magazine of Literature*;

"Caves," *South Dakota Review*; "The Crew," *Southern Humanities Review*; "Conversion," "Sacred Heart," "Host," *Studio* [Australia]; "At Sea," *Talking River Review*; "Hands," *The Third Eye* [reprinted in *Blood to Remember: American Poets on the Holocaust*, 1st Edition]; "By the Window," " In Borders Bookstore Coffee Shop," *Troubadour*; "Bergen-Belsen 2000," *Visions: International*; "After Viewing Max Beckmann's Triptychs," *Wascana Review*; "Penitential," *Windhover*; "Colonel Flogg Weighs In," *Windsor Review*; "Commuting," "The Children Of Bedjin, Poland," *Yet Another Small Magazine*; " Among Wolves," *Zone 3*. "Humbert Humbert's Song," "Judas," and "Lazarus" are from my *Scrimshaw: Citizens of Bone*, published by Lightning Tree Press, Santa Fe, NM.

For Erin, Devin, Pauline, and Annie.
I cannot tell these dancers from the dance.

Table of Contents

Ensemble

Personae

Epilogue

Dedicatory

Apologia: Uncle Fitz

His knees bent stiffly in the oarlocks,
He rowed his rocking chair through gentle waves
As he surveyed the clipped boxwoods,
The mob of tulips nodding between the dogwoods
Where they floated in pastel waterfalls,
The sidewalk whiter than sand, a narrow beachhead
Beside the sleepy street, the mirroring trees
And shrubs around the houses on the other side.

I know what they say, he softly began,
The slick salesmen of intellect and art,
About life here among the small hearts
Staked out like token roses and tomatoes
Or hardening in houses kept too clean
Behind lawns too often mowed, and too green:
Knick-knack lives on shelves.
I can forgive their constricted hearts,
But not their failure of imagination.

I played hard scrabble and did the *danse macabre*
In one pair of shoes from '33 to '35
And two shirts I sewed myself
Rinsed in rivers with names I never learned.
I stole my bread and sold what I could do without,
Worked at everything for nothing
And learned to pass off starving as the flu,
Until I lied myself into apprenticeship
To the dark Satanic mills
Where I worked like the very devil.

At night I read to still my soul.

Then I found a woman who would have me
For half the usual lies—my Anne Marie.
So I built this porch first and then the house
Myself, secondhand brick by brick,
All so I could see a little more life gather
To play tag or blindman's bluff among the leaves
That hung like party ribbons
Or a beaded screen before their faces,

Faces round and smooth as new fruit
Because I gave better than I got
For forty years to a narrow job
Whose joy I manufactured for myself
From dross into fine angles toward a perfect fit,
Not for praise, profit, some passing revolution,
But because I loved—Anne Marie and the brood,
The god I wrestled in the yard,
And the work I found myself bound to do
Because it was mine,

Where I sat as an oily acolyte
To a series of masters bolted to the floor
That showered me with tiny curls of metal
Like silver eyelashes, or flakes of snow
Surprised by bright lights
Before they gathered in my lap in drifts.
These were beautiful and fine.
When I saw the polished edges
Like man and woman fit without a seam,
I learned to dream the dream again

And create the faith that withstands—the tornados
That peeled our roofs like playing cards,
The floods that sent bewildered tables, tires,
Dogs and cats and neighbors
Floating through the streets,
All balky things like our indecisive hearts,
The whole parade of war, disease, and death
That trailed the newsboy on his bike,
Rang us on the phone, or stopped to call,
All to shill us for a hundred lessons
In barely hanging on.

As I hung on one full hour in 1951
To this front door, a telegram in my hand.
Part of me stands there still.
As I hung on later to the bedroom door
Longer and longer so many mornings
Before going in to see her
Pull her beauty back into bone,
Feel the pressure of her fingers
Disappear in mine, see her incandescent eyes
And the wit she strung like Japanese lanterns
Through fifty years of talk, gutter and burn out.

Learning life to be one long goodbye,
I worked overtime to fit the dream
To this old street angled into neat corners
Under elms with broad shoulders
And willows with long, delicate fingers,
For I knew this avenue to be
One dam of driftwood in the stream
Where I could sit a while among my neighbors
To spite this brittle body walled around

By what its hands created, heart endured,
Like every other stubborn citizen
Of this ordinary street.

Prologue

Dawn

Not gently, he comes to her
from behind. They face the cave mouth at dawn.
As the sun spills itself upon the mountains,
he feels in his release incoming light.

Thumb upon the mouth of his bowl,
he presses its lugged curve slowly, rubs
his fingerpad circle after circle,
leans toward it his whole body.

The dying elk's fear thrills him again,
fills his muscles with salt. As he
poises to break its neck, its eyes pin him
 down like hers. Identity troubles his sleep.

Walking at noon, his sunlit skin radiates
warmth in return. He stops. Eyes closed,
he slowly raises his arms. Lifted up,
he thinks of wings. Moaning, he soars.

Once in water slipping on a mossy stone,
he flails until weakness floats him
on the surface, gliding between small
paddlings of his hands, buoyed and calmed.

Visions in sleep lead him through
new worlds rising from the old.
Their pictures compel him to charcoal,
verify in line, copy and create.

He slips around his shoulders the elk's hide,
fits the rack to his head, recalls the meat
filling his stomach with peace. He stoops
and glides: as if. Paws the dust.

Charred bones heaped, he smells their grease
on his fingers. Touches again their smooth sides,
shifts and angles them, clicking, together.
Braids them in a leather rope for his neck.

Moonlight steals color into sleep.
Sunlight fits his children to his sight.
Absence and his first dead woman haunt him
as his hand kneads the flank of this second one.

Weed straw and nettles, his own smells,
repeated days, seasons, stars. The hunt.
Birth and death in blood and silence,
blood and noise. Each breaks in on him,

rubbing their skin against his skin.
Above each moment he sits removed
as each shape circles a center
teasing him like fog, just out of reach.

Adam's Death

—After a poem by Nancy Sullivan

After their voices hoarsened and stuck,
Grated like husks along their throats
And still he failed to move or talk back,
They poked him with fingers and sticks.
The skin merely puckered and went white.
They pulled at his ears and lips,
Flicked with tentative fingertips his blue eyelids
Until one found two flat stones to hold them down
And so disguise his empty stare as sleep.
He could still bleed, they found,
When one's cutting stone slipped its thong
And grazed his stippled thigh,
But the blood flowed heavy, dark, and slow
Across the pale and pimpled skin.
They covered him with signs,
The tracery of fire-hardened sticks:
Natural wonders of trees and stars and rocks,
The shapes of women, designs
Of his own hearth, bowl, and weapons,
Events from his particular past.
Then they dragged him with care across the keep,
Cleared a circle for him with their hands
And with leaf-brooms swept it clean,
Then sat down one by one
To watch him turn to stone.
He informed their eyes all day.
At night they heaped the fire nearby
And tricked themselves with shadows

Ten thousand times: eyelids, fingers,
Toes, lips beneath the shadowy tongues
Of light seemed to strain and shift.
Always they were wrong.
Only his hair and beard combed the wind
As they always had when he stood
Tall to lead the hunt or to speak by the night fire.
When his chest hollowed like a cave
Beneath a steep ladder of ribs
And the rest went slack and stank
Like the old uneaten meat
They could not stand to smell or see,
They threw him away—
Knowing nothing else to do—
Into memory, strangely certain,
As the bog pulled him down
With its remorseless wet hands,
That bad dreams would soon uproot them
From this land.

Into the Bog

Into the old times. Quilting the hides,
eyeing paths just wide enough to scout through,
fear and death immediate salts to breath,
caves of the body to sleep inside.
Desire as clear as the sun: the trail
fat with game, her fingers and lips at once,
spring softening the hills, the gods' wild dance
in the carved rocks, sustaining without fail.

Because down the mountainside a yellow fog
blurs the cave mouth and its tongues of fire.
Stars wheel their knives above the bog
where the bodies cure and turn to leather.
Above slit throats their young features sag
with sleep, weary guarding life forever.

The Body in the Bog

Absolute as this braided noose or slit throat,
the body in the bag remembers.
Each mole and eyelash, every fingerprint

of sleep's neighbor lives on. 2000 years
wear the same ragged clothes. Identical,
time-sprung, as if caught in mid-sentence

about the wheat's tall wealth or some
new neighbor's hips, her golden hair.
His neck wound's lips mock her mouth

of generation, yet his face sags in peace.
Although the tannic acid dyes his dreams
the shade of dried blood, he sleeps

the sleep of the blessed. The scapegoat
is sacred, like the boggy lands.
We must imagine Sisyphus happy,

Camus said, tanned and floating
through the slop of ages, then the grappling
hook scarlet with ideas that won't let us

rest or leave. The soul stutters
when the shell refuses, surrounds him
with the rusty water of a new womb,

pays generation unto generation
the price of perfect memory:
perfect sacrifice.

Caves

In one corner a red hand
says in ochre: I am not here.
I am elsewhere on my legs, my hair
hitting my shoulders as I run.
I am not even bone.

Bison and miniature horse
do not prance along these walls.
The mammoth whose outline follows
so shrewdly the natural clefts and strata
of the rock knee to flank: This mammoth
is not here. Three sabre-toothed tigers
roar in silence, deafening only time.
These tigers are extinct.
They became extinct as soon as they
found themselves confounded by stone.

In firelight, the lines shift and run.
They suggest. Until the fire goes out.
Until the cave's dark breath, ash and damp,
fills every inch like black water.

For I have not walked down this path,
serpentine, barely visible among linden trees,
waist-high grasses, nodding pink and yellow
wildflowers. Down and down to the abrupt
small window in the rock, weed-grown,
irregular. I have not made my way, stooping
through this lost door, to middle earth,
charcoal's death and ochre's blood

survival into all that is
and is not, what escapes
to remain the taut rope between us.

I never found this cave,
30,000 years asleep, painted marrow
her bone retains. Greater than Lascaux,
Chauvet, Grotte Cosquer. Revelation itself
mile after mile. A world, they all say.
A world gone forever back among us,
awake to our arc lights,
microcomputers and spectroscopes.

The past, they say, is not gone. It lives.
It gestures all around us here its color and line,
its textured suspicions made manifest.
Death hesitated here, and died.
30,000 years these coiled muscles waited
to spring, these claws to rake
this bull's flank, these diminutive-hoofed
gazelles to dance again, this red hand
to declare: I grasp this limestone still.

We need only stumble and look up.
Tilt whatever beam we bring with us
overhead, attend to the outline again,
discover and invest. Ague and chill
will not matter, nor the unsuspected cancer.
What we touch here will be enough:
this skinned grace, this deep surface
held up by our common ground.

Lucy

Our strict memory in bone grins here
with relief, free of soft complication at last,
those anxious floodings of blood
and persistent dampenings, pleasure
swelling into pain until she hardly knew
the difference, all the encumbrance of love
long since melted away, sexless
until the experts probe pelvis and shoulder
with calipers and statistics,
their skeletons of lust.

How simple and clean her symmetry:
the embracing ribs, delicate fingers and toes,
the anatomy of love available at last
in every scar of passion and disease.
Here on the hip that drunken slap
against the hut's stone wall the night
her third child was conceived, and his memory
too here in the bend by the birth canal.
The elbow that leaned in wonder
toward the stars above a moon-silvered rock,
knees that scrubbed stone, shoulders bowed
by sheaves and young, fingertips that knew
the green grain from the ripe, and the herb
that cures the poison that it grew beside.
And here is where the world's thoughts
flew in as odor, color, sound
and then flew out again as voice,
articulate clothes we cannot guess,
one more tongue dressed in stone.

Could I pretend so well if yours
were the rosary of bone hung here each day
for the instruction of the crowd
shuffling their gorged veins and tissue
past your trim lines, their tally stick?
No anonymous live birth but Devin Michael
and arthritis, the widow's hump you hate
but have inherited from your mother.

Our embrace would be the same, who always
made room to flesh the image out
all along the naked riggings of desire.
We bury what we cannot bear to see
of love, then become her archeologists,
bereft of all but what we bring forever:
love beyond the bone, and warm imaginings.

Duet

Marriage Reel: Buster Keaton's "Seven Chances"

Veils flying, a thousand would-be brides
chase Buster down wide, nearly empty streets,
his legs a blur but his back awning-pole straight
under his trademark boater. Once his inheritance
hit the papers, its deadline and its marriage clause,
our hero was doomed. So here they come!
Flattening both teams of a football game
despite their thick jerseys and soft-leather helmets.
Now they are emptying the stands,
barreling over home and visitors.
In and out the spark and shuttle of trolley cars.
Into a ditch from which workers pop up like toast.
Over the tracks behind a railway crane
from whose giant fishhook Buster dangles by his belt.
Through a cornfield and beekeeper's village,
unmarried grasshoppers and queens joining in,
all on Buster's heels as he races in then
out of the river, a turtle dangling from his necktie.

On through the shooting range, bullets flying
harmlessly through huge powderpuffs of smoke.
Out into the wild hills, terrifying grouse,
releasing gales of laughter and an avalanche
of papier-mache boulders every size from
baseballs to buildings. The stones want to marry him, too.
But he is a miracle. Treed, ditched, drowned,
cornered, his grainy image in black and white
and gray gets loose in the final reel forever
as he ducks just in time and the androgynous boulders
shoo the women down the valley and Buster races

one last time in his patented sandpiper style
home to Mary his one true love, marriage
and seven million gazoolians against all the odds.

Once more he pays the steep price of laughter,
invests everything in happy endings
frame by frame. He runs down fate with a brakeless
Model T, a swinging ladder, the falling house
crashing around him as he stands upright
in the single open window (a stunt
whose mortal danger studio lore confirms).

Comedy joins us to him and hope forever
and becomes the altar we run to
down aisles of infinite predicament.
We escape together into the mist
of images where the dead appear
and cross the line to greet us, as if film
were spirit, comedy the only death
allowed on Saturday afternoon. Two by two
in the dark, we believe and believe,
even when the ending's eye winks to black.

Epithalamion

—For Pat and Audrey

A walk by the river, its slow turning,
calms their souls down to a summer day,
finds the clock path in their winding

dusty footprints, tangling branches and needs.
Sees in the brown and single tide
mate and lifetime, husband and bride

borne on evenly, two into one
flood beneath shoulders, back, and legs,
buoyant the marriage bed where sun

and moon lie down to die.
Shore to shore each glimpse displays
new folds of light that will not stay.

Joy tells the depths bearing them away.

Dmw-Hlw

My heart leaped up when I beheld
Don and Helen in their Ford
LTD (or Dave and Hilda, Hattie and Doak),
As snug in their respectability
As their fully loaded five-year-old boat
Lumbering safely along the road
Ten miles below the limit,
AAA sticker and Masonic rubric shield
Neatly grouped on the bumper sinister,
All pinfeather clean as Helen herself,
Her blue-gray Civil War Memorial Coif
Aglow in the front seat, a halo of curls
Above her unsmiling face, salt to the pepper
Of her substantial Don sitting six hands away,
His porkpie hat raked low
Above his clear plastic frames
Yellowing around the nose and ears,
Stolid and straight as one of the posts
He sank three feet (exactly) into the ground
At (precisely) 8.3 foot intervals
Around their spotless cottage on Slowpitch Drive
Up from the softball field and nursing home.
In tandem now so many years
It became a downright necessity
To commemorate the fact
With one of those vanity plates
For the back of the car and let them know
That by God here was one marriage
Somebody made work, if only to spite the times.

In the Old Way

We have watched the moon curve and swell
Above so many porches for so many years
She has driven us a bit mad, too,
As we juggle names, dates, houses, whole tiers
Of states with genial incompetence.
It hardly matters. The penance
Of memory is not what holds us here.

When you curved and swelled with children
(Your belly whiter than the moon, the blue
Tracery of veins like rivers seen from the sky;
In sleep, you rested them upon my thigh),
I withdrew too far a while, hurting you
With silence—unfit at twenty-two
For the muddle of so much mystery
Inside my hands and heart.

We face the mysteries together now,
By default of love; even as grandmothers,
Uncles, aunts fall like blackened fruit
And our mothers wither and gray.
(Even with your body by my side
I hear in dreams the sound
The cancer makes as it travels my mother's bones:
The sound of gypsy moths we heard
Only at dusk, as they slew our maple trees
One deck of leaves at a time.)

We see the children grow into themselves,
Flexing their strong legs for flight

And the spring toward other lives
We will never quite admit, or see.
We soon will be left to the fright
Of one another's faces, without the gauze
Of others in between. We can stand the sight,
Having looked before and long
Before the rest could guess
What such long looking saw.
We can pay the penance of decay
With two bits of memory.

For we have loved in the old way—
One day at a time with lots of talk.
Our friends still wonder at our ease,
And so do we. But we know, at last,
Love to be the tease eternal
Which brings all times and seasons
Gently to their knees.

Chinese Lanterns

That fall we gathered the orange pods,
paper tulips on a stick, behind the old house
we just moved into, brightened with stalks
all our new dark corners. Passing by,
we tapped the papier-mache globes,
reverberant as tiny drums.

When we carried our year-old son home
from the hospital, the porch light fell
on the hallway spray. Minutes later,
lapsing sunlight of December dusk
hit the group upon the corner cupboard
where they glowed from within like coals.

Early spring reawakened their wills,
stirred their memories of another life,
tripped the switch in their hearts
so their tiny cannons fired off,
room after room throughout the house,
his head so light upon my arm.

The Operation

Down the hall the surgeon works his will,
And ours, more intimate in two hours
Than I in our quarter century together.
His quick precise strokes add by removing,
The way our love operates upon the time.
In mask and gloves, he probes
Beneath a great silver bell of lights,
Scrapes the scarred surrounding fiber
Before he removes the womb of family,
And so brings up from our foundation
The line between this body and this love.

A gurney like yours rolls up the hall,
Its empty landscape of sheets a flat shore
Where the air flees beyond the horizon.
The time surrounds me like a pressure suit,
Silence trapped in layers against my skin,
My own breathing a mechanical rasp
In my ears, the dry heave of memory.
My slow movements surprise me with grace.

Your pale face floats before me,
Eyes closed in the grave peace
Of the drowned. It is my face,
And through the "invasive procedures"
Of love we are here together again
Beneath the sea, rising slowly hand in hand,
The surface a wandering line above our heads
Where the atmosphere changes, sound rings free,

The chatter of friends, attendant hands
Reaching damply down, a shore crowded with flowers.

Those Who Go Gently

She goes gray among the green plants
Lining all the window sills—wandering Jew
And ladyfan shiffleira, the African violets
She loved as a girl for their exotic promises,
The laddering jade two generations old
Passed on in pieces in a hundred gifts,
Still climbing the window where she swayed
As a bride before the bending wheat,
Long since blossomed into power lines
Above a grid of suburban streets.

He goes quiet as the two cats go,
Treading his slippers across the carpet
As skiers move uphill:
Slowly, with precise imbalance,
Yet lithe as any cat once
He danced on girders where the air thins
And strung suspension bridges like guitars.
Over seven lives ago.

The TV rolls its shadows through the room
Surrounding lives made small and still.
They listen for the shrilling of the phone
To vibrate the house like sirens
From the road. But the black bones
Hunch dumbly by the door. They whisper
Only words no one else can hear.

Soon they will pursue themselves alone
Among the selves they navigate

So softly through their houses,
Floating beyond this living room
Through time and time again
Like the benevolent ghosts
In all the photographs,
All they wore, and were, and cared for,
Even then at the beginning of the world.
Soon, they pray, let me lose all this
And come to myself again.

My Mother and John Keats

Poor Keats coughed up his life at last,
Outdoing my mother by nearly two weeks,
A century and a half, some deathless poems
And an eternal fame he never could have guessed.
Both were full of beauty's tricks.
She was eighty to his twenty-six
And left as her only text the thick outlines
Of four gray children, their uncomposed list
Of memories, a box of sepia photographs,
Another of junk jewelries, scented handkerchiefs,
And a closet full of inexpensive clothes.

I stayed near Keats, too, through the months it took
To live his short life in Bate's long book,
Hungered with him for Fanny and for fame,
Sat up with him, too, when the end came
And Severn's fuddled heroism finally gave way,
As ours did a week ago last Thursday
When the last metronomic rattle stopped
And her last gape for breath trapped
Death inside instead. We said what people say.
But I prayed like Keats for someone to blame.

Now the bone shards and powder—not black or white, but gray—
Lay like a dwarfed thought in a bronze book
Not much larger, lying in the dirt on its back,
Than Bate's *Keats* lying finished on my shelf,
While old phrases from the Bible—the only book
She ever had much use for—dart around us bright and quick
As the snowflakes that sting our cheeks like tears.

The cadence falls and rises on the wind, and my fears
Are older than all of us, older than the words.

Sometimes late at night, when those words rise up
Among the articulate tongues of flame
And the cinders burst like kisses from dead lips,
My text hesitates and heals:
My mother dies in England and the world mourns
In immortal books and poems. A young stranger
Appears one blank February afternoon,
Brilliant with fever and fragile with doom.
His face could be hers sixty years ago,
Mine yesterday, my son's tomorrow.
The wind's brute cold fingers pull at our coats
And hair, freeze the clods of dirt together
Around our freezing feet. The time stalls and waits.
Someone by an open grave begins to speak
And the phrases dare us to draw together:
Love gives beauty its only truth, and truth
Is nowhere near enough. But if life is death
In pieces, death is the life we come to save
In puzzles of words, separate and severe,
Whose harmonies resemble prayer.

Love at Denny's

—For Ed

Waitress wedgies with scuffed tops
and canoe-shaped rubber soles
hove into view, rocking slowly
below trim support-hose pylons.
I am past starving.
Her peach polyester apron and skirt
hug her stomach and hips,
a meringue of golden curls
tops ice-cream cone earrings
and a skewed lace tiara. A chewed
rubber eraser peeks like the tip
of a pink tongue above her left ear.

A reedy voice ticks off the specials—
"Pigs in a Blanket," "Real Men Eat This Quiche,"
"Two Moons Over My Hammy"—tugging
the leash of my dog appetite.
A No. 2 tapping her nose, she considers me
(Cooly. A pro.) through spattered lenses,
then brusquely attacks her order book,
decorating the cake of my heart forever:
"Full burger. Side fries."
The rhythm sprung and hovered
like her fingers through her falling hair.

Walking away, she became
the menu she rehearsed.

Humbert Humbert's Song

Upon these perfect pins stands all
That for a while
I love.

My will tightens
Along each crease
Of her pink shorts;
Her strawberry gum bubbles and pops
On the old stove of my heart.
Each "yeah" and "y'know" sweetly raps
Upon my neural telegraph
Uncluttered sonnets past the reach of art.
Her thighs compress, diverge,
Then merge into her laugh,
A belly laugh.
I love each tune to which her pink toes tap.
Their insipid lyrics light up my life.
In the cradle of her lap,
I rock the past to pieces with delight.
Venus on the half shell,
She rises from my seas at dawn
Erect in all her power
Of buttock, thigh, and fatted calf.

Between her soft covers
I am rolled in the heroic mold.
Her Delft blue eyes tilt me toward
The windmills of the world
As I grasp her yellow mane of hair
And ride beyond redemption.

I am stout Balboa
Straddling twin peaks in Darien,
Come to kiss his dream
Still moist upon the edge of ocean.
Seduced by such sweet science,
I am tireless in my field research:
Triangulating moles,
Graphing dew points of pores
In steep parabolas,
Testing with endless windings
The texture of each hair
Between my caliper fingers;
Testing between micrometer lips
The smallest fact of flesh.
I am willing to be crucified
With bright red nails.

My treatise on Tocharian,
My book on Linear B
Curl in corners like dead skin.
Yesterday a crosswind blew
Fifty folds of manuscript
Right out one open window.
I watched them settle like fat flakes of snow
On the honking traffic far below.

All the idolators of mind
Will never find
The secret secret tucked within
A plowed field of perfect skin,
Hidden between a pair of lips
Pouting like sliced plums,
Never find in footnotes

Such perfect feet
Or hold in all their paper clips
Pages like these thighs
Scrimshawed with microscopic runes
No sublimation can surprise.

I never answer
When they ring me on the phone.
I am much too busy standing here
In robe and slippers
By my kitchen stove,
Whistling Telemann's old tunes
As I brew her cup of tea.

Ballet Lesson

The stoic lovers in ballet
Practice their strict erotic play
Hour after hour, until their youth is gone.
Bodies glance at touch, and tease,
Yet hands do little more than lay
Light fingertips to face and lips.
Muscular arms do little more than lift
And turn, then point with longing
As the partner slips away.

Always the body waits and hides,
Pretends too perfectly, then steps aside
Toward something like the soul—
Apprentice love
Caught forever leaving:
At curtain's close
The body's perfect grieving.

At Sea

My body and I were strangers,
deck-chair mates at best leaning together
above the teak and rosewood slats,
posing for the ladies beside the brass
and cut-glass doors. (He won their hearts
easily, and never lost at shuffleboard.)
We talked without listening, nodded off
when the snapshots came out.
History thickened irregardless.
Sunset glittered off the brass rail.

His regimental smile and blazer
suited our surroundings, like the crease
his flannel trousers kept and the cut
of his badinage. "He had but ever
slenderly known himself," he said of Lear,
silver and crystal rattling past us.
"And after he learned it all, his love
dead in thirds before him, we were
left to sweep the crowded stage."
Lady Fitzpiffle wound her watch.
My monologue on Descartes, though sprinkled
with polite applause after dinner,
mostly flew into the spray or among
the laughing gulls. I often stayed below.

As I pushed him over the stern rail
into waves breaking the moon to pieces,
my momentum revealed, far below,
a white cross upside down, the giant

first letter of the ship's name I always forgot.
As the cards came round to me
at Lord Boodle's table, I wondered
over brandy if I'd sacrificed enough.

Ensemble

Macrame

We are the weavers
Of intricate knots that connect
Around the holes:

Great hooting terminals
Switching massive trains of thought;
Cloverleaves tied into vast bows
To wrap a world of souls;
Trunklines that slither beneath concrete clothes
To form a net of news;
Synaptic flares,
More numerous than stars,
To surround dead space with clues.

Commuting

The delicate crisp of newspapers
Only wrinkles the silence
Until it lies in folds against the skin—
Dead news of another world.
Bodies slump and strain the contours
Of expensive suits
While silk ties billow like the signal flags
Of yachts, toward doubling chins.
A reddening sun
Flecks the dusty windows with fool's gold
Or winks with an amber eye
Through whiskey glasses.
The coach rumbles over rivets
As even as the beats
Of a heart rocked to sleep
Over silver tines
Running parallel, it seems, forever.
A briefcase snaps shut
Like a rifle shot.

A gray-green mobile
Spins by outside like other lives:
A blur of hue
Framed and made safe by glass
And speed and space.

Among Wolves

Howling tilts our ears.
A sprawl of color

rounds the dark street,
narrowing our eyes.

Gray ghosts
circle a fresh kill.

Their morsel
reddens the snow

beneath more howling
and the moon's curved tooth.

Shell Game

—for Ray

Three stories up a plywood shell the color
of maize and wheat, a wing of men carpenter
a luxury townhouse on Ocean Drive.
On the acute pitched roof they stay alive
to make a living, hammering in code
the architect's vision. And ours from the road.
Distant owners wait for windows to rain
attention against, long downspouts to drain
unwanted invitations off roof beams
shingled by then, perfect in every seam.

We can hardly guess the cost: sixteen rooms
ocean-front, custom, easily the tomb
of two million dollars. A vacation
we could nail and brick up but never live in.
Like these daredevil authors, our hired army
nailing shut around us the same old story.

Regret

I hope to tell you we were shocked
At the 89-year old man found dead
Of exposure and malnutrition
In his rat's-nest apartment,
$180,000 in grimy envelopes scattered
Everywhere like old hopes, old sin.
In a local bank they found $300,000 more.

We lifted our 89-year old feet
Onto the brass yacht rail,
Stared past our handmade shoes
Into the rosy pink horizon,
Raised to our withered lips
With liver-spotted hands
Our Remy-Martin and disbelief,
Sip by despairing sip.

The Winners

Imagined from "Harold and Louie," an excerpt of oral
history published in *Harper's*, April 1989.

When we got all the money at first
of course we thought: Wonderful! We could feel
every wish coming true around us,
jumping up like flowers: sports cars blooming
in the driveway, houses taking root
all over the world, it'd all be
prime cut tenderloin, champagne bubbles,
and every dream a dime. Of course that was before
we started getting all these letters,
what with being in all the newspapers
and on the radio and TV. They were terrible.

And they came from all over—France,
Africa, Japan, Switzerland, a place called
Herzegovina. Now who'd think somebody
over there knew us? And they were all up to here
in misery: husbands in jail, electrocuted,
lingering in cancer, cirrhosis, insanity,
so many diseases I never heard of before,
but when I looked them up, there they were.

Children shot, on drugs, stabbed in the movies.
Lifetimes in wheelchairs, iron lungs,
prosthetics that cost more than my old Mack diesel
when she was new. People whose faces melted
like putty in fires and needed years of money

for noses and ears. I could hardly sleep for seeing
these pictures like a movie running through my head.

One little girl was allergic to the whole world
and lived in a bubble suit and special rooms
to keep that one rogue elephant germ
from trumpeting through her veins. One boy
had progeria, which made him look
like the mummy of Methusaleh. In the picture
he stood next to a big rubber Mickey Mouse.

Those two got us both real bad. On and on
and on they came. Heartbreak by the sackfull
dropped its dead weight on our floor each day.
I know what you're thinking. And there were
some phonies, we could tell. But not so many
as you'd think. Most folks don't lie that good.
But after a couple of months it hardly mattered,
the true or the false.

I started smoking again and watching
the all-night movies. My food tasted like dust
and I had trouble talking above a whisper.
We didn't know what to do, so we tried
putting them in piles, worst to best.
Then just children, then below a certain age.
Americans, then just old people like us.
Then old people from our state here.

But there was always too many left out,
no matter what. So in the end we threw them
all away and built a library here in town.
We're supposed to get an award for it

up in New York City but I'm afraid to fly
them jets and we're too old to ride the train.

Seven-Eleven

The gangsters at the mini-mart
sneer and pose, hang danger
from their golden earrings,
flex biceps round with baby fat.

They ogle pink plastic flesh
on the videocassette rack,
grab their crotches and whistle
before the slick covers
of the girlie mags.

Marlboros lit, dangling,
they stab ash toward the floor,
their props perfect: oversized shoes,
tattoos, gang patches on leather sleeves.

"What it means!" one shouts
from the football pages, holding up
a photo of a helmet to the chin,
the receiver's head snapped back
like a bottle cap.

Another rubs his nose and winks,
gestures behind the young girl
buying bread and milk.
A stare from the counterman
turns him, mouth and eyes
wide with fake surprise,
swiveling his hips.

Outside, fluorescent light
burns the padded shoulders
of their black jackets
as they strut, punch
pantomime and laugh.

To be is to be on.
Their white leather high-tops
glow against the asphalt,
each step repeated inside
puddles skimmed by moonlight
and blowing trash.

In Borders Bookstore Coffee Shop

We sit above our coffee
inside walls thick with books.
The second cup is free
at Borders, and the quiet nooks

full of wood and readers.
These muffling words
comfort us. We are feeders
at the crossroads

of bread and print,
tables with silk mums,
croissants, kisses permanent
around a napkin rim,

history deep in the eye
of the matron with the cane,
one crumb upon the doily
of her collar. She entertains

the sandwiched facts
of some eternal feud,
then limps toward the back
for one more cup, freshly brewed.

Late Afternoon

At the rinsed end of the afternoon,
sunlight squeezes clean through the window
dirt, the dog's and baby's moons
of slobber, streaks of cereal and putty.

Three spiral notebook sheets white as milk
flap across the grassless turf and hollows
of rain full of sky. Frayed silk
and cotton underwear lift their knees

toward the power lines. Tilted bikes and one
upended stroller rust under
the roof of aqua fiberglas half-fallen
next door. Wind cracks it like thunder.

Kid cries break out down the alley
and a white tennis ball sails high above
a row of rusty trash cans. One voice talleys
the score. It's something, he says, to love.

Why There Are So Many Murders at the Post Office

All those letter bombs pasted shut
by dry tongues, for one thing:
spring-loaded longing and betrayal,
the old manila bait and switch.
Flat secrets by the ton shifted by towmotor,
loaded in the bomb bays of snub-nosed jeeps
to explode lives barely awake over coffee,
shrapnel for immigrants in their own homes.

The enveloping universe, glue
deserting stamps flown around the world
or railroaded in sailcloth sacks.
Dead letters still unburied.
Everything he will never know
cinched up tight for the long haul,
all in the care of a trained army
uniform in clothes and oath,
sworn to deliver what each one
waits for, paid for, bet his life on.

(Her lips and tongue along the moist edge
follow the contour skillfully,
the soft crush of closure
then her departing fingertips.)

Those damned eagles everywhere —
sleeve and pocket, overnight packets,
vans, stamps, planes. The whole damned country
in his mouth soaring away

and both his lost children swaying
from his talons, all he loves
taped or strung up, still undelivered
and always leaving.

To Have and Have Not: Two Poems from Hollywood

—for Erin

1.
Here in Hollywood he fears
that every lie has already been told.
That among the plastic brick and stone,
matte paintings and towns with false fronts,
room after room without ceilings, plaster,
bearing walls, he will at last feel at home.

Instead, he walks the miles
of corridors through the prop warehouses
and deserted sets: home towns, barns,
courtrooms, streets of cities from all ages.
His elbows knock against styrofoam
holding up the Empire State Building and the Elgin marbles.

Back in the car with his souvenir
film poster, he marvels at his readiness
to believe. Hand tight on the padded wheel,
he pulls out of the studio lot in a flood
of neon and mercury light.
He nudges the pedal carefully forward,
disappearing down Alameda
two red lights at a time.

Perspective swallows him entire,
pulls him deep into the night.

2.
Neon, nudes, and art-nouveau
up and down Hollywood and Sunset.
Bogart and Bacall patrol
the fog around Martinique,
trading dialogue sharp as her hips
beneath the padded shoulders.
Attitude in black and white,
color for the tufted leather green Desoto
cruising these same streets with us
between the devil and the dream.

In her Forties Burbank bungalow
Elizabeth turns blue typing "midnight"
on her mortgaged computer.
Her heroine is a waitress because she
slung hash herself in twelve restaurant/bars
in five years to get here among the images.
In sleep she pans and zooms,
pulls back slowly, lingers, fades.

Bogart winces under his Captain's hat,
pulls a .38 from the desk and kills
the silent man, rescues the loveable rummy
Walter Brennan plays, saves the Free French
couple against his better judgment,
grabs Bacall—who at a lissome twenty-one
he falls for on and off the set—and melts
off the screen. As the people file
up the steep aisles toward doors
wide with sunshine, Elizabeth dreams
an ending at last, a surefire finish

she prays in her sleep to remember
tomorrow and nail down with light.

Three Emigrations

1. The Boy

The eloquence of old photographs
Lies beyond the stilled faces, the bodies
Frozen in gesture, even blurred—
Like this immigrant boy hefting a knapsack
Larger than he is down the fretted gangplank,
In too big a hurry for the old film.
All dead now, these thousand
Milling cells of one great body
On all the decks and up and down
The long docks. Derbies and long dresses,
Mustaches and kerchiefs and shoes like boots,
Crowding everywhere, the tiniest fetus
Snug in the ship of his mother over 110 today.
No, these souls live only here,
In this wink like God's.
Yet they absorb me like neighbors, this boy
Especially, his face lost in haste
Here in his new world and the blur
Of his future. Today our lenses
Would catch him, pin his expression to the page,
But I prefer in him this mystery like mine,
This life still moving in its stillness.

2. People of the Eland

Like the old ones who daubed their dreams
By firelight on the walls of caves,
The charcoal and ochre alive at night,

Chased by flame across the surfaces
Until bison, boar, and eland run again,
In whom beauty survives the skinned pelt,
Charred flesh, and ring of greasy bones.

Only the shaman can become an animal.
But any man can become a shaman
If he can perfect the movements of the dance,
That trance of truth made visible
When mystery's burden is renounced,
When the healer cures with his hands,
Energy flooding his heart and fingertips.

Men in their rattles, holding fly whisks,
Lean in traditional postures to assist him,
His body elongated by the dancing firelight,
His head curving toward the painted stars
For the power to cure, to enter the hearts
Of the animals, the mystery of their life.
When the shaman dies himself,
The eland runs away with his soul.

3. The Man and Woman

Together in this cave with windows,
The TV a phantasm in one corner,
The sound turned off on a *Geographic* special,
Elephants dawdling silently among eucalyptus leaves,
A pride of lions full of gore and sleep.
One turns spiraling antlers between thick paws.
Hallucinotropic sedans and trucks
Fly by outside, my sleeping wife entranced already
Upon the sofa, sealed in quilted cloth,

Adrift on the boat we arrived on,
Empty bags blurring in the attic
Turned to a wall of script,
Representations where we sift the new world
From the slag, the bones and straw of our time.

The Crew

Our withered arms strained as the oarlocks groaned.
Sea-foam riffled our gray heads
Until our beards dripped with sea wrack
Around our tightening smiles:
The rictus of our fate.

The bottom boomed against the waves
Like bone against slate.
The sail luffed and yawned
Until its ragged edges seemed
The fraying beard of one more mariner.
We slid upon the seats like fish
And rowed just to hold to something harder than ourselves.
He said again:
Let your muscles ripple up those tattered sleeves
And fingers study every grain of oar!

Most mad, indeed;
Yet he saw in us the iron arms and eyes
Of old, and made us remember:
What our wives threw off soon after
We lay with them as girls
Among the wild goats and sharp gray rocks
Under that uncanny light:
What our children never knew

He knew of course
Our stooped wives and narrow pensions
Had grown as stale in their turn
As his baffled ambition.

The grandchildren in their smocks and lace
Were dear, to be sure;
But indulgence soon had run its course.
We had pulled the world in our wake
Once. The world!
Yet now a glazed mirror
Sought to forge upon history a spectre
Grizzled and lame, gray and harmless as a dove;
We who had thought death himself love
Once, so taut had life been strained
Against the spar.

So we went.
Gladly. More mad by far than he,
Buoyed as he was by destiny.
Bewildered tears and rage
Broiled around the pier.
Angry women, embarrassed sons,
Daughters with stern faces dandling young ones
Milled about distractedly.
But we knew. More than ever now
As the wind spun and swelled the sails
Above our gray faces
And the rope rubbed our hands raw
Once more.

Drum

—for Fred Stefon

In the drum
Swales the rhythm of the hills
That fall from the eye like scales,
The wind that runs like a horse
Between them
And among the raindrops who dance
On eyelids and lips,
Who hold with wet hands
The hair upon my neck
Until it runs a thousand rivers
Down the deep-rooted world.

In the drum
Swells the heart of the seed corn
And the hearts of the spotted horses,
The dark, curving bellies of women
And the hearts of young men born
For the women and the spotted horses,
As they run between the raindrops
Big as fists
Falling from thunderheads
Who growl and roll above the hills
And are the drums of god.

In the drum
Fly the hands of women threshing grain,
Slapping the dough of sweet corn cakes,
Speed the footfalls of racing boys,

The puffs of dust that rise
Behind their pumping knees,
In the drum
Is heard the quiver and thud of arrows
One by one like the notes of song
Upon the pitted practice tree,
Felt in the sting of string
Across the back of the hand
And in the rise and fall, like the line of hills,
The evening story travels
Around the uplifted arms of fire,
Raising into life the voices
Of the dead.

In the drum
I hear the snort, like breaking ice,
And see the frozen breath of the buffalo,
Still as a black stone
Above his knees in snow,
And feel his great heart—
Larger than my young son's head—
Beat winter into spring
Even as I feel beneath his heavy hide
The slim arms of my wife
Holding winter from our door.

In the drum
Ripens the hope of rain
To crater summer dust
And brim in earthen bowls,
Collect in pools
Around the tight sides of seeds
Before they shrivel like the women's lips,

Cracking their curves with blood
Until the drum unties the cords of sky
And rain runs down to cool
The fever of their faces,
Pulls green shoots from the ground
And pelts like tiny hammers
The dry belly of the drum.

In the drum
Sway the hips of all women,
Lush with appetite in early spring,
And the eternal dream of seasons
The dancing women bring
Wrapped in their slender fingers,
The rhythm of the great wheel
Of the land and its times
Upon whose broad back
The fathers of our fathers danced
And where my foot resounds again
Beside the light foot of my son
Between the rain
Resounding rhythm
From the drum.

House Sparrows in October

The fall flocks loot the year one last time,
Rifling the leaves, darting tree to tree
In arrows of anxious hunger,
Ready to bolt, uneasy in their hollow bones
With gathering instinct: Tomorrow or tomorrow
We will fill the skies with wings
And perfectly connected energies
Until we quiet our nature with new homes,
Barely perceiving the journey once we land.
Now we celebrate small lives of faith
In food and breath and generation,
A conviction that is life itself
Embraced in the ecstasy of song.

Whale Rood

Once more the beached whales refuse their lives.
The men, their own lives raw in their hands
And burning with salt, work against the tides.
Winches and pulleys groan, small boats with ropes
Pull the slack tails that lay like dying butterflies
From the beginning of the world. Shoulders in waves
Move young ones back to the sea where others spill
Sea water on their heads in small christenings of hope.

Always they slip away, return their placid bulk
To the shore, settle themselves upon the land
Where instinct beaches in one funeral collapse,
Grinds into sand before the cameras
One grim bulletin from the invisible sea:
See how we lay this burden at your door.
Observe the breath you deem the whole
Grow shallow and end beneath our own weight.

Women and children along the shore mourn
For the gentle humpbacks looming before them
In shapes of their own dreams. Their own desires,
Promptings of flesh resolving into flesh,
Lay dying before them, without hands to grasp
Or words to bear. Only the salt smell of the sea
Revives them, the steady pulse of waves
In their veins, and the laughing gulls.

Wearying more than their backs and legs,
The men cast about to net this rogue miracle:
A virus of the inner ear persuades the whales

That this air is but a paler sea, giddy and pure.
Slack magnetic fields reroute their maps,
Or storms so silt them with debris they cannot gauge
The surfaces or monitor the deeps.
Thick films of garbage toxify the plankton,
Or dreams of harpoons toxify their hearts.
The intricate empty net will never fill.

On the horizon of the sea, a toy ship
Sails as slowly as the moon across the sky.
Its napkin sail wipes most of a world away,
Even as the morning blue daubed the moon
Up like a spot, now a fingerprint overhead.
Dunes hide the city, barely half-awake
Above a coffee cup, the news still rolled
Outside the door, or so much static on the radio.

We come here for you in our long, dying lines.
Over and over our songs in the seafold
Echoed, strange beckoning waves to you
Waiting on the echoing shore. As moonlight plies
The surfaces, our singing rings the depths
With ribbons of music, trails of intention.
Now called to more, we sail beyond the spacious rooms
We lived in to this narrow strake of sand
For you to see and measure, deliberate and judge.
Too vast for you to manage, too insistent
For you to resist with life, our great fatality
Mortises with love the land and sea.

Lift

Gravity, said the old man, is the truce
joy keeps with pain. The coefficient
of drag for dried mud dreaming itself air.
Our highly specific density.

That's why we prepare to fly
by shrinking, forgetting, dying off.
Pale hair, transparent skin, rusty tools,
each precious diminishment of flesh.

Nothing but this light shelf of bone,
cunning glider of complete desire
to lift us nearly weightless toward the sky,
the precipice welcome because the wind has room,

delicate cage of guy wires and struts
singing in the slightest gust,
arms wide, hands cupped and tilted,
fleshless but polished with poised

light to ride these thermals to the sun.

The Children of Bedjin, Poland

The slaughtered children of Bedjin
have come back in age-softened photos:
grouped before a school, in twos and threes
with their arms linked, standing at attention
before a kneeling mother, her own young face
smiling above a shoulder, one after another
alone in the center of blue cards
rubber-stamped with black eagles,
tracked with the blotted graceful script
of another time. All gathered together
on our television, with cellos and narration.

Annie has fallen asleep, but I know
we must make room, draw from two dimensions
life enough for three, as the survivor
from Bedjin who made and narrated the film
has done—nearly an old woman herself now,
youth a flat dimension she must believe in,
facts about faces long since bone,
memory whitening like a winter sky.
So she moves pictures through music
and the echoes of her own voice, creates again
a small percent of what was, gives them her own life.

Now they are back, where will they sleep?
What will they wear? An extra school bus
will be needed every morning. And how will
my wife and I afford them, pensioners so quickly
getting up in years? We will do what we must do.
But they are so many. Thank God no one is more patient

than the dead. They will wait as we learn
to listen with their ears, record whatever
they can still bring with them,
live with them the lives they never left.

Photograph of Bergen-Belsen, 1945

These rich shades, pasteled by the lens or morning mist,
Blur expectations out of place already
After all the grainy horrors, the inadmissible truths
In black and white that pierce like barbed wire—
Sleepwalking dwarfs and skeletons, lines of freight cars
Whose broken slats once bloomed with fingers,
Bulldozer drivers in surgical masks
Striving in self-defense to bury the past,
Greasy clouds above fields of snowy carrion.
This odd exposure captures something less, and more.

The single flatbed wagon filled with naked corpses
Sits right-center by itself, a memory in transit.
Grecoesque, the dead cling to one another
And refuse to horrify—in their rapt dignity
Like paschal candles or bolts of ivory silk.
Fastidiously, their genitals and faces
Turn from the camera toward anonymity.
The war has ended here. On the lush grass of spring
A sprinkling of Americans in darker green
Smoke at their ease. But space grows between them
And no one speaks. They consider the lens
With noncommittal faces, these veterans of death.

A waist-high brick fence divides the foreground
From the barbed-wire fence and corn field beyond.
All the rest is open, empty, serene.
Leaning upon the fence, a few more stragglers
Stare in while trying not to stare.
Not one looks at the dead. Studied indifference

Draws the quick and dead together, as if murder
killed all identity.

This held instant distances all the rest.
Of the 30,000 dead the Allies found, only these few
Perhaps remain. Nor do these in their seraphic calm
Resemble those kept whole, as if by onionskin and thread,
Who crowded the earliest burials, the ten mass graves
Brimming with nameless thousands—entombed this time
By the death's-head guard themselves, yeasty men and women
Made to handle for once their zero sum of evil.

The Gologothas of clothing, gold fillings, and hair
Gone long ago, no more in view than the other thousands,
The living and barely living. The 200 children
The camp contained sent away to feed their memories.
The local citizens lined up behind the city council
And the burghermeister, visitors at last
To the metropolis of death they denied so long,
Even when the lie fell in black snow upon their fields,
Then stank and soured in their mouths.
All gone except these few.

And these dead will not wait long. They bid the living haste.
These young Americans bore all this heavy news
In their arms and hearts, but their thoughts
Remain as distant as the thoughts of the dead.
They wear the blank disguise of combat soldiers
Everywhere, the ritual mask of the dead,
More out of place here with the burden of their lives
Than the dead could ever be. On this trimmed lawn
Set off like a tiny pleasure ground,
They ought to wear a woman on their arms,

Swing a wicker basket filled with pears,
Camembert, a fine chilled Rhine.

And in the end, what should anyone expect
When men murder for a cigarette
Or scrap of rotten bread, or just to kill an hour?
They who had held life so long against the trigger
Might well die to death, find no spirit left to feel
These pale presences vainly haunting lives
They had given over months or even years ago.
But no. They consider the considering lens,
Transposed by another kind of knowledge.

In the springtime light, the composed bodies
Glow from within, pull the available light
Into their thin shelves of flesh until the air
Vibrates with the luminous ivory depth
Of vigil candles ranged across an altar cloth.
The soldiers' faces, ruddy as the candle flames,
Complete the service here, redeeming and redeemed.
For an aching beauty animates this scene,
One conventional pieties cannot still.

By some trick of perspective, or of art,
Some extravagant promise of belief
Or blundering insight of the heart,
Even horror is not final. Reconciled by exhaustion
Into peace, time gives over even violence
To beauty, lifts her up as the final sacrifice
Once the litter on the stage has been removed.
And the actors, living or dead,
Are left alone forever with their thoughts.

Bergen-Belsen 2000

We have seen you dragged merrily
    from the trucks into the great pit,
    nodding and grinning over the gray-green wool,
    forty pounds of mischief for the cameras.
We elect the hangdog faces of the death's-head guard,
    the wide hips of their women.
We believe your number, not your name.
We refuse these joke-shells you litter our memories with.
We will stop payment on your uncountable millions.
Your continent of ghastly dolls
    will not tempt us to play with you
    among the cows and fields and thatched villages
    just beyond the barbed wire.
We will not make ragged sails
    of your clothes so you can float
    among the swans and rowboats on the lake.
We will not tuck you into the bottom of our wicker baskets
    with the wine, gruyere, pears, and linen.
We will no longer dress you in crinolines and striped pants,
    prop you up against the trees, plastic teacups
    in your hands, bandannas flipping
    breezes through your sockets.
We will not talk for you anymore.
Do not ask us to carry you any further.
We have burned, buried, baled.
We will not barter any more.
We have hushed each grinning mouth with dirt
    and still you echo soundlessly.
We will not play with you anymore.
We are bored and it looks like rain.

We are spooling up the wire and repacking
    the tea set and food.
We will forget you until we get home
    between clean sheets smelling of sun and soap
    when we will reach for you to hold us
    but you, naughty ones, will be nowhere to be found.

Easter Island

Inexplicable stone faces
angle toward the shore,
its tufts of weeds, black basalt
slag of the eternal sea.

Rites hide forever
behind steep foreheads,
family resemblances
of woe and insight.

Dragged across pea-coal turf
by carts, by hundreds, by a faith
moving mountains
but carving them first.

Gone. Wind and guano and silence.
We stand beneath their long brows
and noses. They wish for hands
and shoulders to shrug.

We wish for stone hearts
below the surface of the ground
on a level with the sea.

Kumbh Mela

The boatmen on the Ganges
Charge eighty times the normal rate
When the holy men swarm her flanks
At Kumbh Mela, when immortality
Runs over their bodies in tongues
Of water, when the planets' promises
Grow less invisible, and sins lie sunk
Beneath her brown surfaces.
Many come naked, renouncing all
But dust and ash. The billionaire industrialist
Maneuvers nonetheless a private interview
In his hut on stilts above the beach
With the holiest of the holy men.
600,000 per hour stream toward salvation,
Their goods piled upon their heads,
While the most orthodox celebrate
Their own funerals on the shore—the death
Of their former selves. When the body
Complies, no further rites will be required.
They will bob like cork upon the Ganges.
One pilgrim has held his arms aloft
Eleven years, the muscles long since atrophied
In penance. Another has not lain down
Or sat for eight years of the promised twelve.
Nor will he speak. 'He sings songs to God,'
His bearded familiar says: 'What else could he do?'
Some of these, says another holy man,
Do not do penance properly anymore,
But only for the money of Kumbh Mela.
He does not say what God pays

Of the difference. At night arc lights
Flood the sand with saffron piety.
The parade will resume tomorrow.
Among the millions, two toothless women
Who will not see Kumbh Mela again
In this form send incense rods
In circles before their withered breasts,
Their eyes turned so far toward heaven
That only the whites can be seen.

Sacred Heart

They always return together now.

Our weekly practice hiding under our coats
in the hallway as the streetcorner siren
wailed all hope out of us, second-graders
of the Cold War who watched on our little TVs
white mist rise eerily from the ground
before the shock wave collapsed the frame house
over and over again, then the rather
beautiful cloud umbrella opening slowly
over the world's head that somehow made us
hide our own between our hands,
kneeling in a line under coats hanging from
rows of hooks the emptied souls of childhood.

And the deepening hole just beyond
our classroom window where the new Church
of the Sacred Heart was soon to rise,
once they finally got through the rock
stubborn and deep on the corner of Walnut
and Mary Streets, so they would blast
early in the afternoons, rattling the panes
while our heads were down on our desks,
low concussive shocks that made
Mary Alice wet herself and a few others cry
even though these frights did not require the hall
where our coats barely shook on their brass knobs.

We learned the word *explode*
so we could understand: the way X marked a spot

for the rest of the word to blow away,
to build up by tearing down, but soon
we forgot as we watched the steeple
rise and heard the bell tested directly
across the corner from the yellow siren
squat as a gourd on its telephone pole
that no one took down till we were grown
and gone, long since communicants between
green pews and mosaic-modern stained glass,
long since slapped gently by the bishop,
confirmed one and all into the mysteries.

Communion

This perfect idea
presses humbly on my tongue,
dissolves without trace
like bells rung
into mind
one moment past
or from unsteepled ages
dark and slow
who built fingers in rungs
above the thumb
so others might lay stone
in rows, braid bell-ropes
for bells they learned
to cast and pour
until they healed dumb air
with sound

dissolve without trace
into the word,
living lip and tongue
redeeming air
and the porched ear,
invisible flesh
into flesh
and song

without trace
into the continent
of the body,
rivers and countries

teeming the shores
of the felt hours,
the cells that come and go

too distant now the cell
opening on a garden
of silence,
unrung bells heavy
on their hinges,
their hips motionless
inside the wet morning,
faith a presence,
the breath
lifting his chest,
walking the cedared paths
of sense
into the matins of mind,
fitting a world
to itself,
ringing in
the dawn of flesh,
sustaining it
with bread.

Host

One by one they approach.
The aisles slur with their slow movements.
Warm breath touches my forefinger
and thumb. Our eyes touch first,
a foundation for the words,
contact where the blessing identifies
us, too: "The Body of Christ."

Into hands callused by work,
neutral as iron under the disc,
a dime for the vale of scars.
Vast as a pocket watch in the child's fist.
Softer than the summer moon
in the branches of this elderly hand,
barely warm above the outline of bone.

Impossibly, I am the vehicle for
this moment we recognize together,
give and receive to realize
we cannot know who gives, who receives,
cannot separate the body
from its bone, the soul, its head
from its hands. We consume the horrors
flattened and bleached, changed
by what we can, and cannot, see.

Personae

Vaudeville: A Time-Step

Sometimes I think my life was only
ten minutes long, my sister Kitty's, five.
We were twins, and in the stink of the stage —
sweat, garlic, cigar smoke, old clothes,
and sawdust — we were born. And there was blood enough.
Little June more than once rinsed it
from her toe shoes. The Nicholas Brothers
swabbed it from their taps. Everything wooden
buckled and split. Sleep was shaking trains and back seats.

Perfect memory killed vaudeville.
Our ten minutes down cold in the hot lights.
All the rest hurtling around our still center,
the act. Our unstill center: claps, whistles,
even the busy dead silence some nights.
Then the films perfected imitation.
At last we could rest.

We counted on lights and distance
to cover the sweat stains and frays,
our own smells we danced and joked in.
The act surrounded us. It was us.
Slips and garbled lines, the night Kitty sneezed
through it all, only kept the act clear.
We sang or wheezed the same, paper suitcases
packed with everything we needed, but always leaving.
"You kids got a good act," Mr. Rosenfeld said.
"Don't change a thing. I'll get you on the circuit."

We practiced even harder, tightening our cues,

our identities, tap and tune a single seam,
while our tights pinched and our bodies bloomed.
Some nights I danced and seemed to watch myself
as if I sat alone in the balcony,
studying the act through the smoke, lamplight,
shifting chairs, coughs, trolleys rattling by outside.
What new still center now? I thought, hovering
between what I realized, and did.

Once the movies flattened us against the wall,
only a few stayed on or made it big.
It was too late to love change.
It seemed to me that all I ever knew
hung weightless in a beam of yellow light.

Once, as the old woman I am now,
Kitty dead before the war, I watched TV
one night and saw on PBS a show on Vaudeville.
And there we were. Fifteen seconds
in our Maryjanes and shiny frocks,
Kitty and I going all out across the scratched film.
I never knew it existed. I watched
in a dream. Then I bought the tape.

I still don't know where we were or when it was.
I know the curtain was orange like our bows.
That's about all. It's the middle of our number
and each time the clip ends my mind follows
right through to the end. The opening is gone.
Kitty I can never see enough of.

In my little garden the lupins dance,
the woods beyond a stage set seen from behind,

the sun a spot going out, the house not empty
yet because you had to stay to see the last act.
Near the end, we closed for almost two months.
Our outfits clung with sweat and the men
whistled and stamped. But the act never changed.
That was the strangest thing, when everything
around it came and went. And still is.
I just wish they'd have caught Kitty's full smile.
But that never came till we took our bow.

Jason

The Glock, its titanium-plastic shell
the color of a golf club, the size of a cell phone,
was perfect, and the bullets were perfect,
perfect when they rubbed together in his palm,
copper bronze gleamings as they tumbled
then lined up tight as soldiers
perfectly in order in the clip which slipped
into place with the rich authority
of a Mercedes driver-side door.

He had no choice, he kept saying
over and over, afraid that he had.
Once the grip had warmed to his body heat
and molded to his hand because the leap
of his arm, the flash and flat dull bark
could never be entirely real, either,
he could say I love you, Mother,
before the five rounds found their way
to her temples and forehead,
and because it was true, he covered her
with a sheet just as he had his father.

They would never understand now (again)
because there was no understanding,
only rain, sun, moon, girls with long hair,
pictures of things pretending to happen
because this was the real TV show
with less pretty people, just clumsy sad people
like himself who just wanted to die
but not really, who had to pull the stiff trigger

until it became a hair-trigger
aimed exactly at the heart where it
came together for a moment, the toxins
on one side, the oxygenated cells on the other,
all together on the same red tide
here in the mystery chamber itself
one moment, united like his father
and mother, only their feet, their
sensible shoes, peeking from the sheet,

that instant where the two people
became another person and the clean cell
and the dirty cell passed each other
or stuck for at least one round
in the revolving doors of Gloucester High
where you could settle the whole thing
once and for all because what else
could you do. You hit the endless repeat
cycle and turned the opera music up full
because you knew it would never be
endless at all, even if no one ever came,
which they would, and the plastic and rubber,
the metal and cones and chips, circuitry
and pulsations of electricity
would wear down soon enough, the singer's voice
crack in the heat, lug and groan, there would be
a few or many mechanical pops,
clicks, fuse flashes maybe, then even
the little red light would go out
and the gray metal case could relax
its corners because it would all stop
and soon no one would ever know anything.

A Biography

First I blamed the night.
Then the moon's false light
and the rising tide of anglers,
each wave hooked tight.

I catalogued the dangers
by the shore. Perfect strangers.
Nets and draglines torn.
The absence of tanagers.

So I founded a city to be born
or die in. Rhapsody of horns
and sirens. Days and nights
a blur loud and forlorn.

Despair took my height
and tied the knot.
Drove into my back
her high-heeled foot

and mailed me to the sticks.
Weeds, gravel, mud-stuck
tractors and trucks. Tethered
me in the chicken shack

among the dung and feathers,
ammonia and ether,
beaks and wings in my face
and cackling laughter.

I tried each pinched face
on behind the octagonal maze.
Discovered the delights
of corn, brief flight, pecked eyes.

Relief flooded my nights
where I held on tight.
Overflowed with tossed
grain in the morning light.

My pimpled bulk dressed
behind sloping glass
on the butcher's tray,
I watch the people pass

with eyes of bone and yellow
skin. Lean and dumb, I know
nothing to misconstrue.
I am my father's son.

Ready to go home.

Bear

Heavy with sleep
and falling, autumn
tightens deep

around this pawing heart,
a cave closing away
blood and memory.

Everywhere in season,
I dream these billion
red and yellow leaves

go off like guns.

The Reader

In great pain he seeks
the order of the printed word,
the steady fencing of ideas
and weeks, punctuation
graceful as swallows
between the corn where phrases
ripen green conclusions,

quietly as the bronze man
on his bronze bench outside
the newspaper office downtown,
intent upon his bronze headline,
quizzed only by stray pigeons.
We are silenced by a heartache
so great as to freeze him here.

For Betsy Fishman

"Little Betsy Fishman suffers from a rare
disease: she is severely allergic to almost
everything in the modern world. Among her
typical reactions are screaming fits and nausea.
'She is like a universal reactor,' one doctor
says. Her prognosis is not good."

—From a news item

When the fever rose
My belly rolled
Over and over.
They said I had no choice.
I had to leave behind
The things I loved
In the old mirror
On my bedroom wall
Where I watched my body
Break apart.
I don't need it now.
My heart will never break.
It bends too well.
But I wish I had a name
For the taste like pennies
Always in my mouth
And the sour milk
I always smell.

I backed away
On tiptoe
To this quiet eggshell world:

One big room
Blank and white,
Where the air comes in
Through rubber hoses
In tiny whispers.
People visit me each night.
At least their faces do.
They fill the tiny windows
High up on the wall.
They talk to me
In little mouse voices
Grated through a cone
Beside the door.
Each time they speak
It vibrates like a heart.

I don't talk now,
Only write.
Words once crowded
Around my face
Like winter breath,
But I think they had
Poison seeds
I breathed in again.
They pinch off my throat
Like a rope of lies.

I write, and wait.
The words on paper
Burn like steam,
To get them down
Harrowing my heart.
Each day I slip

What's left of me
In slices out the narrow slot
Cut like a mouth on hinges
In the middle of my door.

Amish Farmer

Mattock. Helve. Hame. Coulter and hitch.
Earth beneath the cadence of John Lapp's
talk hits like sunlight off a furrow

neat from the plow, clean and damp
enough to mirror the hour perfectly,
what it felt and was filled with.

He cultivates each turn. His spade scrapes
though clay grains, yaws on a stone,
creaks under the last heel thrust.

Dumped, the silver tip made bright
with work stands upright, shivering
in the ground it leveled to understand.

Gymnast

Sleek as otter or lynx
She vaults near the lights
That hang in cages from the ceiling,
Arcs in perfect flight
Her physical insights
Or tumbles their echoes across the floor.
Beneath her taut sheath,
Barely containing
The thin convention of skin,
She ripples with life
Like our original sea.
Not erotic, only perfect,
Her material soul can stretch
My fabric of desire
Until it threatens every seam

Arcing through my echoing vaults
Here among the gawking crowd,
One of the attentive bears who hulk and yearn
For flesh so fitted with its own idea
That to move is but to think out loud

But will settle for well-muscled words
Poised for impossible springs
Between immovable bars,
Arms and legs drilled deep
Into the heart,
Angled knees and elbows swept in curves
Above all beams wooden and inert,
All bars too parallel

And iron rings too cold,
To find the flight above them all
That unsentences the soul,
When the word rises from the killing floor
To dance through a woman's limbs
In single celebration: the grace
That settles over skin.

After Viewing Max Beckmann's Triptychs

Like the rest of us
Beckmann lived upon the echoes.
Sent them rocking down German rails
three freight cars at a time.

Like the rest of us he built
simplicities to hold them in.
To hold them up to view.
One, two, three hinged boards.

Like us he pretended
triptychs into altars,
stained-glass cartoons
from the Church of the Shallow Grave.

Like us he prayed there
to lift from the junk
of his own past—Norse kings,
schoolrooms, odalisques blowing bubbles,

victims like us of almost everything—
the blood of their right colors
between fat black lines,
tie them to stakes

to stand them up like us
in families, straight ahead
down the aisle from the narthex.
One, two, three

angel wings closed like our
hands before our faces.
Lock the many into one
until tomorrow's doors

open on a woman tied like us
to her lover, upside down,
a man without hands
reaching for the sky.

Snap shut like our hearts
before the blood pulse
beats again, or stops
forever. It does both here.

So we would assemble,
dye without dying
if we could. Cover our eyes
and stop our ears with paint,

catch ourselves in one
elegant wrecked torso,
 stare them down all day
then close our hinges

with our invisible hands.

St. Francis by the Lower Lavatory: St. Joseph-In-The-Hills Retreat House

"All bad art begins in genuine feeling." —Oscar Wilde

The kindly saint crushes a blackbird.
No, a robin, still struggling in his hand.
A dove, perhaps just preceding him
in death, plummets softly past his knees.
Other barely recognizable birds—
a jay, cardinal, kingfisher—
look dubiously up at him.

At his blotched cheeks, flattened nose,
chin wide and dimpled as a knee,
an expression somewhere between
rhapsody, rant, and imbecility.
Each eye points ever so slightly
away from its neighbor, and the viewer.
In his upraised left hand
he holds a prayerbook of some kind
which his wandering left eye seems
furtively to consult for what to do next.
Around his burlap robe a rosary
cinctures him, its last long vertical links
and cross hanging miraculously,
to judge from its shadow,
six inches out from his body.

Spilled soap runs across the blue flooring
of the sky. Turrets with red tops like minarets
pass for Italy. Brazilian rain forest

foliage, bloated and strange,
frame the good man in his ministry

so at one with earth and earth's God,
the great Lover's lover,
near-perfect likeness to the art
life paints wings to reach, tiny hearts
shuddering too fast for anything but flight,
colored to mate with the eye
as well as one another, to overfill
our canvas with the image of divinity.

"Are you in line?" a man asks
as I stare. I step farther away,
looking for the signature.
I cannot make it out, of course,
though the brass plaque records
that this dear monstrosity, all five
by four paint-by-numbers feet of it,
was the gift of Dr. and Mrs. Somebody
In Loving Memory of Somebody Else.
Warily scanning the corridor up and down,
I lean toward a particular blur
of bamboo leaf, log, or cassock
in the left hand corner,
and trace a name I know well
with a flourish of my index finger,
bumping over brushmarks
almost to the wingtip of the falling dove.

Conditional

The day's music escaped him,
perhaps because the old man crashed
through his back fence only to throw away
his crutches before the police handcuffed him —
forgot them in the kitchen, in fact —
as he had the small python on his torn
back seat, in a glass cage, although the snake slept
peacefully enough and continued to molt.

He had watched calmly enough
as the old man sailed past, doll-sized
behind the wheel, straight off the driveway's curve
over the arbor vitae and petunias and the fence,
although the old wooden slats were so soft
with decay they flattened almost without a sound,
and the car shuddered to a halt just before
the lower yard's 3-foot drop. We all assumed
the brakes gave out but no one ever checked.

The police were polite, clean-cut,
self-consciously male. Everyone pitied
the old man despite his tattoos and Harley shirt
because he said he was a totally disabled veteran
and wore Velcro sneakers, had heart trouble,
barely weighed 100 pounds, and drove
a dented twenty-seven-year-old LeMans wagon

the color of weak cocoa, although nobody
could believe a word he said after he claimed
he had a lot of money at home and the City police

showed up while the Township police
were still there, bearing a bad checks warrant
for $150 worth of candy, especially after
he walked so well, even handcuffed,

forgetting the crutches. He looked sick enough,
weak enough to have just come from the Veterans'
Hospital as he claimed, just as his car's lack
of a license plate might have been because the plate
was stolen, though the officers could never find
the report he said he made. Although
mistakes certainly happen. Evidence is lost.

And his new car, a 40K Aurora,
might have been in for its 5,000 mile checkup,
and his home could have been a 250K cottage
on the Susquehanna, although we all doubted it
because pattern was all we had,
and a flattened fence, gray wool uniforms,
an old station wagon with a folded wheelchair
and a snake all together in the upper yard.

"Thanks, Mister. Thanks, Mister," the old man said.
"I just turned in here to get off the highway.
I'm sorry. Real sorry." Grateful that the man
was too stunned and sorry and fascinated
to be angry, carrying the crutches as he helped
the old man down the steps again and into
the squad car, and was soon alone with the LeMans,
snake, former shrubs and split rail fence.

So the music was, at best, tentative,
the notes bent somewhere toward comedy –

like when the old man held his forearms up
to keep the cuffs from falling off
because his wrists were so thin.
A little like Bill Frissell's weirdly wonderful
atonal take on country ballads he heard
later that evening – oddly unresolved
although the old man's eyes,
barely visible inside the white bush
of his hair and beard, looked back at him
from the squad car window with a look
so gentle he had to smile himself,
at which the old man winked and gave him a thumbs-up,
the handcuffs sliding up to his elbows.

By the Window

—"Humility is endless," *East Coker*

Brace-pegs tight inside the rocker base,
routed and lacquered posts, brass pins
around the beige velvet backpiece convince
Grandma of the near embrace of grace.

Feet slightly above the floor as her weight
sinks back, she lifts her knees,
grips instinctively the velvet sleeves,
feels the weightlessness of weight

before she smiles forward, grey eyes and hair
catching the light, her broken slippers flat
on the rug, ankles already arching her feet
to try again that sacred inch of air.

One Body

Heart and blood pressure, bladder and ear
infections, irritable bowel, Parkinson's
and metabolic rate: Grandma gathers in her
tiny plastic cups the day's ration

of pills—this morning's measure
anyway—as neatly as she surveys
with her Bic her weekly calendar
to see whose turn's come up: which duchy

of the body and its reigning magistrate
she must attend to with busing
schedules folded in her purse. Never late,
she ordains another day for living

through waiting rooms, depot toilets, and rain.
Cranberry juice every morning. Never
touch spices or nuts. Shingles last June.
Spastic colon spastically. Her bladder

an inoperable sagging glove
clinging to disease. Erratic heartbeats
indifferent to her hates and loves.
Hiatal hernia. Thank God for Tagamet

and Medicare, drugs on the discount plan.
Three novenas and daily rosaries
won't let this chalice pass away. Wine
each morning, bread to nourish mysteries.

Host to too much life, she is the good thief
of days. The altar cloth breaks over the corner
marble squarely, and the priest's wide sleeves
rise evenly each time he prays for her

and all of us. "The body will prolapse, scar,
 convulse, thin too far the blood it offers
up and diet down to crusts and wafers.
Offered up for you." Amen, she quavers.

And tries to kneel.

Grandma on Wash Day

While she naps in the wing chair,
the load she fed piece by soiled piece
into the bin of the rotary washer

rumbles from the basement and shivers
her dreams. Keeping clean is hard work.
So she scrubbed her soul every Saturday

since that day at twenty-four
when the white sheets on the line
hung eternity's drapes around her,

rose in wings from the ground and sang.
For fifty years the slotted window
slid back upon the low tide of her sins.

An unforgiving thought, a barbed word,
an old desire where he leaned
against a fence-post. So she hazards

perfection a few minutes more, asleep
above the filth beneath her feet.

Sight Line

She found the stranger again,
this time as she adjusted one curl
close to her mirror, and with her left eye
saw her left eye seeing

blank as the deer head on the pub
wall, so busy letting in light
unchanged, she could not recognize
herself as someone seeing

until she went back, curl
to fingertip to wedding ring, small
because they were poor then,
seen now as clearly

as sorrow, as joy, and reflection
flew back to the hazel eye,
floated across its dark diameter,
sank slowly down the well

without end of everything she saw.

Snow Man

He seems well suited to this place.
Still and severe, he is all attention
To the hard facts, the inflexible case,

The rigors of a world of frost.
New snow slants against his back,
Restoring what he has lost

To time's runes and scars.
Each day he shoulders down with woe,
Contracts beneath her signatures.

At night his crystals lean and lock.
Intent beside the empty road,
He overhears our dreaming block

Talk in its sleep of June,
A green intention
Left for dead one November afternoon.

We attend him one by one,
For his counsel hardens privately.
He understands the silences of bone.

Some say in ecstasy he hears
Cold comfort coming down. Some say
He feels the trade winds lifting near.

Yet always to silence he returns,
The shape of cold, and death, and nought,

His wordless crucifixion by the storm

Whose traces fly and drift in everywhere,
Thickening evidence
Too icy to the touch to bear

Until we satisfy the soul
(To say nothing of the heart)
With dead twigs, more silence, two lumps of coal.

May: First Take

Every bird has a microphone? Good.
Set designers and graphic artists
finished? Super. These green things
glisten like wet paint, don't they?
Whoever thought to haul in these big trees
with the white shoelaces and poofs, and these
short ones with those pink-and- white, softball-
sized blossoms: good job. Get his name.
And this turf could be real.
The nip in the air is almost perfect,
but cut the wind a tad. Her hair, you know.
When the Spirit of Spring appears
we want her see-through tulle to ripple
like an erotic flag but not fly over her head.
I don't think she should talk, no.
Just let her glide around, shimmering,
stretching gracefully, stooping strategically
above those yellow—daffodils?—OK, they'll do—
then in front of the—right, forsythia.
Let them whip her gently. Keep us on the edge.
Then she'll just disappear through the woods,
looking back at us with a complex look,
"full of meaning" as they used to say,
sort of hating to leave us, still enticing,
and then something else, something for "depth,"
you know, something a little lost, I think.

The Near-Seduction of Professor Kling

The signposts are out: Dangerous Beauties
Today in West Chester. The students gone, sunshine
insinuating perfectly: giving us ideas.

Seventy degrees, late May leaves laughing
together before old gray stone,
streets dozing in shade: they should be grieving.

Our skin disappears. We go all pore and portal.
Reflection goes on spring break and writes home:
Of course. Now. 7:46 A.M. Not that birth canal

carnival ride, permafrost years, her geologic death
to the seven-year August of bone cancer.
No memories hooked to each nerve. This fat breath

of early summer instead, hits of ether
in an early morning gel-cap or syringe,
hope a green thing in dirt, oblivion *du jour*.

Colonel Flogg Weighs In

They have their nerve you ask me
These suicides taking up the news
Young ones especially every day.
Tough for them getting a date
Friday night and frying burgers
After school. And those lawns to cut
On Saturday. No wonder they hang it up
A life like that. Live a little I say
Make dying worth something
When you really need it, crooked with diseases
As many scraps of lint in your shorts
Like me you've earned the right
To milk a .44 Magnum and paint
A modern mural with yourself
Against the wall. Best idea you ever had then
Till they scrub it down and wheel you out
With your nose pointing straight up.

Of course what do these kids care
The whole world's in a selfish hurry.
Pansies. Oh God they cut me from the team.
Lordy Lord I knocked up Debbie Sue.
(Most creative thing she'll ever do too.)
What's the use of living. Let them uncurl
Like a scrap of paper every morning
Like me and beat some blood
Into their legs with a broomhandle
They can oil the bearings of my wheelchair.
But nothing works out like it should.
They just better never try it over here

In my yard the little cowards.
I find one dangling dead ripe
From my prize quince some fine morning
There'll be hell to pay.

Groundhog

Sour breath and spite
Heave this mood along,

Pendulous belly
Barely above ground,

Red eyes busily aslant,
But only for grubs and roots

In musty houses under logs.
Birds are songs he never sees,

The sky some brighter patch
Lying crooked on the ground.

Breath torments his chest
Like the old footprints

Troubling his mind
With muddy suspicions

That he will never fly
This gloom of rock,

Moldered limbs, or buryings,
That even with wings

And wind, an eye
For the journey, shavings

Of song in a rapid heart,
Muscle and skill to lift

This bulk into the sky,
Still he would not try.

Conversion

Into the black bible the boy poured
the dusty streets, their voices sawtoothed
through the wooden evenings the sun
charred slowly but could not consume.

The cheap cloth cover bowed and cracked,
red page-ends water stained and ran.
He guessed, sounded out. Rhythm
counted off the hours, seeded the green

lawns, leafed the trees, echoed
the rain against the corrugated roof,
tamed his breath upon the bed where he lay
listening, phrase on phrase, truth enough

to root the time in voice, closure
in syntax, line, and page. Sound pursed
his spirit inward. Vibration released him
into fenceposts, streets, faces

all around him that refused to leave.
He became the glass of his windowpanes,
roof and hearth against the winter tongues,
beginning, middle, and end.

He began, he thought, to understand.
Until the onion-skin pages hardened
to mica and took hammer strokes to crack,
rag to wood pulp to stone polished

in the stores to hang from ropes
and chains around their necks.
He went back outside, at last eighteen,
letting the brisk wind spin the leaves

soft as down again. They flew up in wings.

Penitential

Deaf as wood to wisdom
I angle into the kneeler
my bent life, polish off
sins until they dance

walnut candle flames
around me, captive heat
shimmering the walls
of my small house.

Doused sin inside
a votive jar smolders on,
one snuffed trail rising
black through the red light.

The kneeler groans
with old guilt,
royal purple kneed
by sorrow and relief.

Christ falls three times
along the walls,
hangs above the altar
all afternoon

poised incarnate
marble, my eternity.
Behind the sanctuary lamp
shaking its hips

in the wind, he winks.
I confess all I know,
hold the future in
against the past,

grip the crosses
carved in the walnut sides
in case I rise, winging
away too far, too soon.

Emeritus: A Grammar of Assent

One of the "eminent dinosaurs" am I, John?
Well, leaving Dean Mallard's politesse behind
(His either-ended smile), I've half an "aye"
To give the epithet. Lately the woods
Seem thicker, and my bulk extends beyond my breath;
A brontosaurial heaviness weighs
Down my thoughts, indeed. The museum may be next.
Scut! Let him do his worst. I'm half past caring
And tired to the very bone. The dregs of my
Ambition could be stored in the bottom
Of his coffee cup. And his Young Turks bore
And anger me by turns with their febrile
Self-concern, their politics, that most odd
Pomposity of youth. Lord let them rise
And be a name: the chiefest feather
On Stephen Duck, John Clare the Water Poet's
Raft and oar, all Grub Street's kennel broom!

Lord save us, John! Either I deserve the toe
Of your glossy English boot, or else my dotage
Opens up a new career: curmudgeon.
And why not? God knows they need a scourge.
I could whittle a stout shillelagh,
Don my academic gown and mortarboard,
Roam the halls to rail against the times
And pillory the bureaucrats, the shallow
Snobs, the blank pragmatic young
With their statistical souls—striking at night
(My gown aloft) to torch these dungheaps
Of computer cards, jargon, illiterate reports;

Deans, Bursars, and Vice-Presidents would lie
In clumps, their eyes locked in their weasel stares
Forever, a neat red "F" between them.
Quietus causa? A heart thrust with a cheap Bic pen.
(Nothing over nineteen cents; I'll need a lot.)
The Luddite of Literature rides again.

Too late, John, much too late. How does that mucker
  Mallard put it? "Retrenchment requires...
Accountability (of course: the ledger sheet)...
Years of distinguished service...perhaps a rest
Well-earned...Enrollment, at the best,
For medieval studies, after all...."
The hypocrite: His ducats and my daughter.
Yet it was not always so, and more and more
I find myself needing to remember.

Do you recall the Greek Revival tower?
(God, no! Not that penile shaft on the square,
The Trustees' Freudian whimsy.)
No, this one stood by the old Lyceum
In a small grove with benches—gone years ago.
It had the most resonant carillon,
Pealing matins, vespers; so they seemed, at least,
To me, standing by this window listening
While the sun sat in that gnarled tree—gone now,
Too, I see. Strange! only to notice now.
Sprinkled students were trysting or reading,
Unlike those hurrying ones below.
Those notes seemed somehow to ring out over years,
Along the rough coast of an ancient sea.
I almost felt the ceinture round my waist,
The weight of my woolen cloak, wet from the sea wrack;

145

Heard the scrape of vellum; smelled the incense smoke.
At dusk I stood watch for Columba's sail
Upon the stormy Irish sea—so drunk
With hope and the music of vocation:

> The rasp of keys in many locks,
> The chain-weight heaving from the hasp
>   to the ringing floor,
> The sweet heft of vast, priceless books
>   to men bent upon the timeless chore
> Of love: illumination.

> Sunlight falls from the latticed heights
> Of narrow casements
>   into pools of liquid gold,
> Sets fire to crimson vials, more red
>   than the memories of lips,
> Burnishing plates of molten emeralds
>   with an ecstasy of tints.

> Across the stiff vellum
> Meticulous brushes move like needles
>   with infinite deliberation,
> Scoring mere skin with beauty,
>   and forcing from slow time
> A living memory:
> A moment when love and faith
>   held poor wisdom close.

Forgive an old man his ration of romance,
But I've begun to know the dancer from the dance;
And images of late too real
For memory trouble my sight, my soul.

Almost all dead now, John, but you, and each
Glimpse over years more uncertain or false
Than the one before: even dear Mary's face
Forced now to live merely among my nerves and bones.
Enough. Or too much. Although I have not
Miles anymore to go before I sleep,
I do have a class to try to reach,
If I can.

McClain

Above the husks of sycamore,
shavings in trails along the ground,
new skin shadows the forsaken place.
More grows invisibly underneath.
Solidifies. Loosens. Peels.

Shasta daisies unfurl in the plots
where the more expensive perennials
were slain by the rabbits and birds.
Nipped stalks. Their beautiful heads
disappeared. All their memories of color.

Near Gettysburg, an ancient greenhouse
stands from 1865, its remaining panes
glass plate negatives of the war
long ago rinsed by the sun.
Awakened by their moonlit ghosts,

I watched *The Civil War* again
to learn to assemble the still scenes.
Interweave the right music and quotations.
Learn to live beside McClain, who moved
from Bull Run to Appomattox Court House

only to find himself the registrar
of the beginning and the end.
Home and family uprooted to escape
all that will not be moved. He leans against
a sycamore, shasta daisies by his feet.

The Visit

Who am I standing here, sixty years
A shadow running along the ground, haunting
Again the outside of my home where it stands rooted
Beneath the slowly rocking linden leaves,
Full of strangers, its white stucco recently freshened,
The wide slats of the front door thick with varnish.
I grow in place today and drink deep
From the horror of this quiet sunlit street.

Not Kristallnacht only, when their faces
Like red meat above the brown butcher's wrap
Of their shirts discolored and ran
As they dismembered with their axes
The soul of this house, and struck the first
Deep strokes inside my life. One blade swing
Grazed mother's ankle before she could pull
Her leg beneath her on the bed. Not that only.

Or the Channel voyage, the chaos of the camps
Brimming with refugees, the volunteers
Overwhelmed but struggling to be kind,
The foster parents before the Simpsons
Whose name, Whourry, rhymed with sorry,
All the black nights of sirens and tears,
The letters that still found me occasionally.
"Be a good girl. We think of you always

And trust our loving God to put things right.
In time we know we will see you soon."
The English of that last line touches me still

While so much worse has fallen away.
I have been up the front walk, on the verge
Of the single top step, then stopped.
Once I saw my hand reach for the brass ring,
But the age lines, the old relief map of veins,

Held me back. Of its own accord, my body stopped,
Stilled by the oddness of its own life. Then my own
Children grown and gone rose up before me,
And Mother long dead who came once in a dream—
My photograph pinned next to her heart at Dachau—
To find a daughter grown into a stranger.
We stared wordlessly, our shuttered hearts
Almost too quiet for memory to bear,

Merely neighbors of the night. Now all this time.
So this warm breeze inherits my face,
The silence of this knoll where I can look
Toward my parents' bedroom window,
All the thoughts that refuse to come.
I shed them all from the empty fingers
By which I held on, dropping the world
Like a coin into the crosstown bus.

Hands: Abraham Kunstler

Cursed with a body
Stronger than stone,
I lived on, and on,
And do so still, prisoner
Of some dull will and purpose
Buried under skin.
Starvation
Only hollowed every muscle
Into sharper definition.
Doomed at seventeen
To endure in blood and vein
The powerful shell of man,
I became the stranger
Hidden in each pair of hands,
The stranger in my own.
"Iron Cross" they called me,
Salting praise with irony—
I a Jew in recent flesh
Become the spade of Jews beyond redemption,
My iron arms outstretched
Like the heavy wings of earth,
To gather in the dead.

For twenty-seven months
I lugged the guts of other Jews, Gypsies,
Communists, morons with their cow eyes,
The old, lame, sick, at last
Anyone at all,
In wagons, trucks, wheelbarrows,
Many times by hand,

Their soft parts bouncing on the rutted frost,
In spring carving like coulters
Shallow furrows in the mud,
Sliding with odd grace
Until they tumbled, broken, down the sides of pits
And all grace collapsed in heaps.
Legs and arms and backs would snap
Like dead trees in a storm,
And more than once one going down head first
Would break his neck and turn
To fix me with dead eyes.
Women and men tangled
In a parody of love.

So many shades inscribed
The page of flesh:
The bleached chalk of bone,
A gray sky pregnant with snow,
The golden yellow of a finger of wheat.
(Like teeth, one dental student said,
Though only dentists notice.
And only we and lovers, I thought,
While I could think.)
All rolled into my net
Eighteen hours every day—
The flat bellies of starving fish
On a tide that only grew,
As if each body were a cell
And the sea of flesh a cancer.
While I could think,
It seemed a world was dying
But could never quite be done.

By the time the ovens rose
Like churches with small steeples,
The wave had washed away distinction.
Age and disease,
A spirit folded like a letter in a purse
And meant for someone else,
Or signed over like a will
Too soon: these gave way to young women
With bellies still round with hope,
Men heavy with health
As if they still had lives to lead
And somewhere to walk to on strong legs,
Children delicate as orchids
With hands like petals.
I bore them all
As the labor of my hands.

I shoveled till my shovel broke
And dragged until muscles turned to brine,
Turned green and choked
On Zyklon B from going in too soon,
Found lesions bleeding on my hands.
The ovens stripped my eyebrows, arms,
And half my head of hair,
Branded my face with permanent fever
And burned my retina past repair.
Today the world appears to me
A watercolor over gray.
Taste and smell were sanded down the same,
Though nothing but more death
Will unbend and break
The stubborn fingers of my memory.

I pushed in all the other hands I knew
But one pale boy, tiny as a seed,
Not yet fifteen, whose three months' work
Came just before the end
When the Americans arrived
 To vomit and to stare,
Who thought perhaps beyond our gates
God left no more for them to see.
They had young hands and faces.
Some no doubt still had souls.

For nearly forty years I kept
With a fine hand all the ledger books
For a small firm on the Neue Strasse.
We specialized in art supplies.
Every day I ran my pale blue numbers
As intricate and thin as fingerprints
In perfect order page after columned page
Without error or tedium,
Quite alone.
Retirement merely hollows my time
Deeper into the palms of my hands,
Becoming one more thing to hold
Without complaint.
With no hint of weakness or disease,
This body bears it much the same.

I bury myself in chores about the house.
In my garden, I tend my crops
In even rows, lush and beautiful.
Flowers I must imagine, though.
Somehow their heavy scent gets through,
Like a finger down my throat.

I remember how the spade shook my hands
When I turned my first crop down,
Crimping their bright heads with the shovel tip,
Stopping up their ears with earth.
Now I make my own with silk and twine
From pictures in my books.
Sometimes I catch in oil
My delicate creations,
Then hang the still life on the wall
Above the flower vase original.
The effect greatly pleases me.

Lazarus

Now my life dances to disappear
Upon my tongue and fingertips,
Past the curtains of my nose and ears
And the gauze before my eyes.
My mind waits on a wooden bench apart.

The leading-up remains with me
In bold strokes, the gravure of skin and bone:
My body like a fired iron
Pressing the pallet with a weight
Like all flesh gathered in one man of stone,
My fever searing the linen,
Sweating into steam
(So at least sensation made it seem).
To call you with one finger curled
No tighter than your longest ring of hair
Spilled acid oceans in my eyes
And stunned me into rigid sleep—
A sleep whose thunderhead of dreams
Told instinct to expect the storm.
Then one afternoon the sun fell into my head, my heart,
Melting every bone with pain.
And then...I cannot say.
I saw two ragged lines below your eyes
And felt them channel mine like scars.
I can see them even now.
Those he failed to take away.

Sometimes I seem to feel or see or hear
The round weighted coins upon my eyes, the muffled bells

Of voices and clumsy shuffle of feet,
One grasping cry thrust up like a spear,
The cool moist of oil sliding perfume on
The scraping scent of laundered cloth,
The ride uneven over lurching ground
Into dead air smothering with cold,
A silence come alive once the grating roar of stone
Sealed itself, and died.
Then a growing lemon slice of sky,
The weight of coins falling
Past my ears, their ring upon the floor,
Groans of a boulder moving
And the dribble of smaller stones among the dust,
The gauze brightening before my eyes,
The first breath shaking my chest like a fist
Until it falls like the sun into my heart
And softens my bones with life.
I cannot be sure.
What I remember seems a kiss,
Two bodies forgotten into one.

Forgotten in his eyes,
I thought, as he stood motionless as any stone
Within the surging crowd, his eyes
On me at war with our necessary lies.
My faltering steps stuttered toward you both,
My mind reeling to its knees
Like the swooning crowd beating their breasts
And souls in ecstasies of fear or joy (I could not tell)
Until in loving dread you led me home
to bury me deep within your warm tomb of arms.

Here in this olive shade, whittling alone

The green wood of my time—
My knife and fingers stuck with sap,
Or by the brown river lost
At school among the silver arcs of fish,
Lingering above my bowl of lamb,
Or in the wicker frail your arms can weave
To hold me fast as we renew
Our youth beneath a once-familiar moon,
I start and tremble on the edge
Of storms which never come.
I find only instants blown away
Past blue puzzle pieces cut from the sky by olive leaves,
Or lingering like memories
In water, a fish's tail before my eye
After the sinuous fish is gone,
Or like the tang of earth ripening for years
In flocks into the meat melting on my tongue,
Or in your lips turned into a taste
Between citrus and the heavy musk of dates,
Your skin into a combed field of grain
Where my fingers run, like boys, forever.

This body I wear like old clothes
You feel cold at times. I see in your eyes
The dead man in your arms.
Yet we have sealed the mystery
With kisses
And learned to haunt our fingertips
Like ghosts.

Judas

"Lawyer," they joked. "Scrollmaker."
As if to read and think betrayed instead of bound
Together, as if to be the hound
Of meaning and worry the brush for clues
Along the crooked scent of truth
Were not the purple and the crown of man.
Such was their simplicity,
They could never see relation, choice, complexity.
At best they petted me with one free hand
While they chatted past me round the fire,
Like a dog they kept for sport
But never sent to field
Because they never knew the game.
I smiled and watched the time
Without resentment. They would never see.
And I was too thrilled
By the chase and chance of history.

He lived among my dreams deeper than desire,
Mingled like breath about my being,
Folded my sinew into praying hands
And swelled my heart with my doom of blood.
Each look, each word
Became the bones that held me up.
As on those bitter nights when the mist stood
In walls around our meager fire
And our hearts ached like our feet
With stones of ignorance and doubt,
He would talk us into palaces
And beds of down until, drunk with promises

And trust, we slept like children
On dead ground.

Once, on the salt sea
In our rough boat, he stood
Like a picture in the prow
And wove the sea and sky together
With words. His hair shivered
As if the fingers of a girl
Had just released it strand by strand
And his cloak fell in sculptor's folds
Below his shoulders.
When he cupped the wind
Between his hands,
The slotted sea rose up, curled
In whiter ringlets and lifted all of us,
Then froze the world one timeless breath—
Before it so slapped and shook the hull
We pitched from our seats like dolls.
That moment, one at balance on the scales of death,
I like an artist felt forever.

How could I fail to fight against
What I alone could see?
The wreck of all upon these local rocks,
His death hanging in his eyes
Like curtains in a window,
Each of us a corpse stiff and twisting in a tree,
With so much left to do,
He in his prime and all so well begun.
Could I let such promise slip into the trough
Of politics, become a gristled bone
For the starving dogs of faction?

Be ground into mush
By the stone wheel of a worn-out law?
Or wash into sewers through the dull greed of Rome?
Only to find *my* promises
Swept off the temple floor next day
Like so much tainted straw.
That money burned my palm like thirty glowing coals
And stunk in my nostrils
Like the dung of thirty mules.
(I flung it to earth among olive trees.)
I only wanted more.
More time to burn the rust
From our benighted country, and ourselves,
Guarantee the future with a plan,
Declare our proofs, research and organize.
More time to understand.

Love alone hated me.
He left me only life:
A bag with a drawstring like a noose
Dropped down a midnight well
Or scattered like seed under olive trees
When the wind kicked the crowd's angry voice
Like a child's ball to and fro
And bent their torchlights down.
One voice rolling from Jerusalem
To pound my head in waves of blood.
Love in that purple grove felt like hate,
Heavy as the bag of flesh I could not pinch off
Soon enough with hemp, to strangle thoughts
That tasted once like mint-silver drops
But now melted on my swelling tongue
Like wafers of decaying meat.

Old Airman

The canopy of his small rancher
tight to his shoulders and face,
he feels the hard floor solder
his feet to this time and place.

The view from the window
banks beyond the picture frame
without him. Yet its slow
bloom and crash he can name

as he names the children
up and flown, the wires that tug
light to the TV, the phone
that once bent miles like a twig,

this world he pins on, too uniform
to cover the nakedness
of weight, time without chloroform,
the quonset hut where the airbase

used to sit, one curved memory
welded shut on every seam
where he lifted off from 1943
into this airless dream.

An Absence of Whales

On the grim ladder of years
he climbs, alone into the air,
heavy laboring hams like wheels,
slow probing footfalls.

Bent hands pin rung by rung
and pull. Slow as stone he crawls,
a glacial song no longer sung
except by solitary whales

climbing their rungs of waves
into northern seas, slaves
to the motion he yearns
for, weary in their turn

with seasons, pilot songs
that dart away like fish.
He dreams of fins like wings
laddering the air. He swims in ash.

Snap Shot

He sits by the ruins of his life,
the steep green expanse, the lone Abbey wall
and half turret full of late afternoon.
Lichen frames the one arched altar window
around a landscape he once loved:
small bridge and hurtling stream,
sprinklings of gorse thorn and bloom,
round fallings of hills into mist and distance.

Unless it was a photo. Glendalough,
St. Kevin's monastery he toured once,
the bus choughing by the roadside
 and the driver lounging behind a smoke
as they walked and stared.
A trip taken and recorded, filed away
behind the gloss of a Kodak print.

Lighter by half, he climbs
the two steep stairs into the kitchen,
hears the hydraulic doors slap shut behind him,
finds a window seat to doze in
and begins to dream of supper.

Epitaph

I tried, by God.

Built till it fell
back to sod.
Riddled with nails
the petrified wood.

Leveled and plumbed
until it succumbed
to wind, rain, dream.

Measured once
and cut twice.

Braided the thatch
and when it dried
struck the match.

Pedaled the bellows
to blow the glass.
Blew out each window
with the .22.

Watched each season
disinherit the last.

I just did what they all do.

Epilogue

In the Garden

for Bobbie Kevelson

"The important thing is not to think much but to
love much, and so do that which best stirs you
to love."
                              —St. Teresa of Avila

Each day the old man clipped a leaf,
held it first among its neighbors
on the tree or shrub, comparing
without judgment, picturing the whole.

Then a closer look in the sun.
Margins, leaf base, and stem.
Lobes by number and size.
Midrib to main and secondary veins.

April through October he would lose
whole afternoons above a pinoak,
red maple, bigtooth aspen,
herringboned hawthorn or sweetgum.

Slow fingerings in his darkened room,
plastic spring into autumn leather,
parsing sound, odor, texture
as he rubbed and bent them tenderly,

waxy cuticle moistening his thumb,
scent filling his fingerprints.

169

Then on to the radiant lights
of his worktable, hand-held lens

and microscope crowding the stage
with personality in strands
of spider web, insect egg,
drought burn, tooth mark of caterpillar

or gypsy moth, each particularity
sung now in chorus with sense
and memory, a life fallen leaf by leaf
into the garden of humility.

Old Wood

I would choose, he said, for my final afternoon
A quiet pub slowly filling up with smoke
Aromatic as the burning leaves
Of ancient Eastern trees;
A pub of old mahogany,
Dark and heavy as the weight of another time,
Rubbed to a glow by endless backs and knees,
By slow stories and civility;
A pub with sawdust on the floor
And the sweet smell of spilled beer,
Where an old man gnarled like hickory
Would turn to me above his pipe
And say:

"I have seen my dreams
Gather like mist in the tangled boughs of trees
Then burn off with the sun of each new day;
At dusk I wrote down their forms and themes
As the clouds curled in again."

Michael D. Riley's first book of poems, *Scrimshaw: Citizens of Bone*, was published by The Lightning Tree Press in Santa Fe, NM. *Circling the Stones* (poems from Ireland), appeared in January 2008 from Creighton University Press. *Ashore Here*, a meditative collection with a seashore setting, is in production at March Street Press. He has poems in two recent anthologies, *Irish American Poetry from the Eighteenth Century to the Present* and *Blood to Remember: American Poets on the Holocaust*. His poems have appeared in many periodicals, including *Poetry, Poetry Ireland Review, South Carolina Review, Cumberland Poetry Review, The Fiddlehead, Arizona Quarterly*, and *Southern Humanities Review*. He is Professor of English at Penn State Berks in Reading, PA. He lives in Lancaster, PA with his canonized wife, Anne. His two grown children, Erin Beth and Devin Michael, escaped to families of their own some years ago.

Printed in the United States
141868LV00001B/122/P